Frozen waters

Beach

Dolphins

Strange sea creatures

This baby shark is hiding inside the book. Can you find him in every scene?

Deep sea

Whale sharks are the biggest fish in the ocean. They are huge but completely harmless to humans.

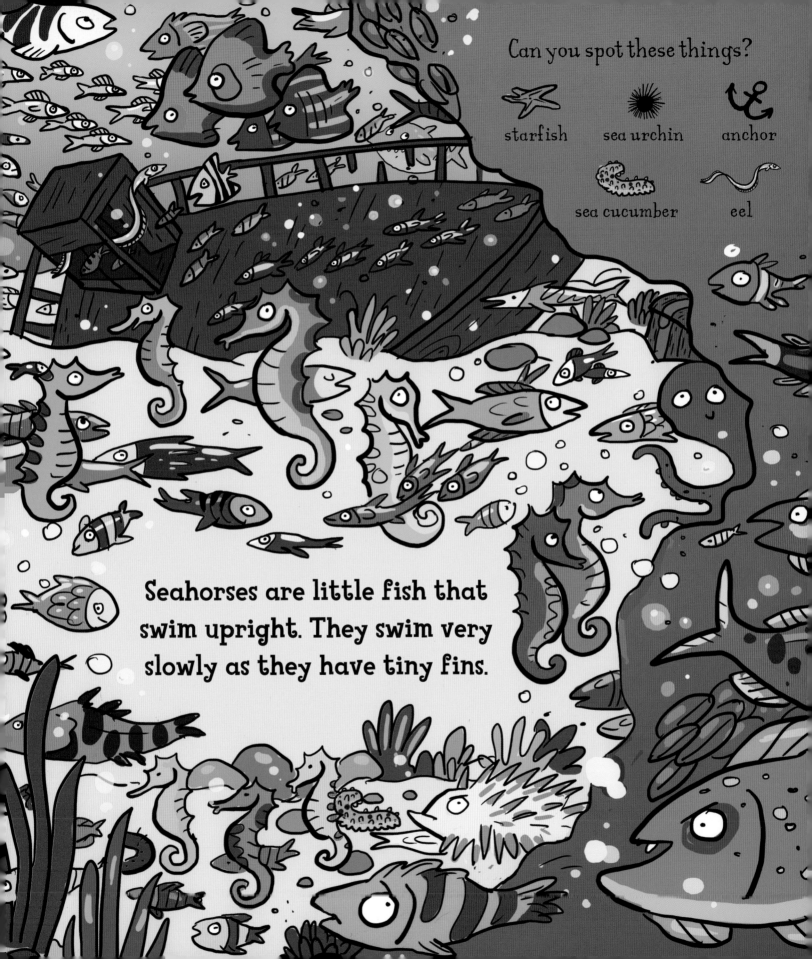

Can you spot these things?

starfish　　sea urchin　　anchor

sea cucumber　　eel

Seahorses are little fish that swim upright. They swim very slowly as they have tiny fins.

Some of the most beautiful fish in the world live on the Great Barrier Reef near Australia.

Can you spot these things?

arctic hare   seal   white whale

arctic fox   reindeer

Turtles live in the ocean but they lay their eggs on the beach. When the baby turtles hatch they have to crawl to the sea!

Can you spot these things?

sign   lizard   pelican   pink shell   blue crab

Some ocean creatures look very strange indeed!

Can you spot these things?

blobfish pufferfish yeti crab monkfish parrot fish

Octopuses can change their colour to blend in with their surroundings.

There is no sunlight in the deep ocean, but some creatures glow in the dark!

Scientists have only explored a tiny part of the underwater world!

Can you spot these things?

anglerfish

vampire squid

red jellyfish

dumbo octopus

frilled shark

Dolphins are very clever.
They leap and splash just
for fun, and will even make
friends with people.

Can you spot these things?

swordfish   purple boat   sunhat   palm tree   flag

More to spot
Go back and find these scenes in the book!

Did you find me?

Did you Know?

There are probably millions of sea creatures still waiting to be discovered!

Penguins and polar bears live at opposite ends of the world. Polar bears live in the far north and most penguins live in the south.

The blue whale is the largest animal that has ever lived. It is bigger than even the largest dinosaur!

Seahorses get their name because they look like tiny horses with their arched neck, long nose and mane-like fins.

Starfish aren't actually fish - they do not have gills, fins or a backbone.

More ocean fun!

Design a sea creature

Draw the outline of a sea creature on a sheet of paper. It could be a starfish, whale or whatever you like! Use pens, crayons or paints to make it as colourful as possible. Don't forget to give your creature a name.

Hide and seek

Choose a cuddly toy to hide around your home for a friend or family member to spot, just like the shark in the book! You could hide other objects and make a list of things to find.

Play 'flip the kipper'

Draw and cut out some big paper fish – one for each player. Line them up on the floor ready to race. Each player hits behind their 'kipper' with a rolled up newspaper to make it flip and move towards the finishing line.

Ocean night light

Glue bits of blue and green tissue paper over the outside of an empty jam jar. Cut out and glue on tissue paper fish in different colours. Decorate with glitter. Put a battery-operated night light inside the jar and turn it on!

Designer: Krina Patel
Editor: Tasha Percy
Editorial Director: Victoria Garrard
Art Director: Laura Roberts-Jensen

Copyright © QED Publishing 2014

First published in the UK in 2014 by
QED Publishing
Part of The Quarto Group
The Old Brewery,
6 Blundell Street,
London, N7 9BH

www.qed-publishing.co.uk

A catalogue record for this book is available from the British Library.

ISBN 978 1 78171 655 7

Printed in China